ENNEAGRAM

*Embrace Your Potential and
Overcome Your Weak Points*

with
Enneagram Exercises, Meditations and Questions

by Eleanor Cooper

entertainment purposes only. All effort has been executed to present accurate, up to date, and reliable, complete information. No warranties of any kind are declared or implied. Readers acknowledge that the author is not engaging in the rendering of legal, financial, medical or professional advice. The content within this book has been derived from various sources. Please consult a licensed professional before attempting any techniques outlined in this book.

By reading this document, the reader agrees that under no circumstances are is the author responsible for any losses, direct or indirect, which are incurred as a result of the use of information contained within this document, including, but not limited to, —errors, omissions, or inaccuracies.

Table of Contents

About the Author

When we were young, no one told Eleanor she need not understand life to live it fully, and I think she wouldn't believe it if they'd have done so. Since our childhood, she was always the quiet girl who saw the world in her unique perspective. Back then, the other kids saw her different, at least at first, but I always saw her as the wisest person I knew.

Her love story with Enneagram started during her work at the university. At first, she got into learning about Enneagram to have a better understanding of the people she deals with daily, but soon she looked inward. That was a turning point in her life.

After several years of feeling different, and getting more and more distant from others because of her way of thinking and her emotional distance, she suddenly had the gift of realization that nothing is wrong with her. She recognized that both the things she loved about herself and the things she felt different about, belong to the Observers, the Type 5s.

From then, she saw her uniqueness as a gift; she learnt to accept herself and live her life fulfilled as a Type 5 (which now she's proud of). Enneagram became a journey to understand herself and find her bliss and a mission to help others live their lives fully.

Elliott Cooper

Introduction

I would like to take this opportunity to thank you for purchasing this book, "Enneagram: Embrace Your Potential and Overcome Your Weak Points with Enneagram Exercises, Meditations and Questions."

Have you ever been surprised by how some things predicted through numerology or horoscope turn out so accurate? Well, you will be amazed to know how precisely the Enneagram can describe your personality. Long ago, it was considered to be a powerful tool for personality growth. An Enneagram can throw light on your strengths and weaknesses, thereby allowing you to concentrate on improving your ideal personality. This can lead to a content and satisfied personal and professional life.

You can take an Enneagram Personality test to determine your personality from the nine distinct types. Knowing your Enneagram type can be a remarkable experience, as each personality type has a distinctive way of behaving and thinking based on the inner patterns and motivational factors. When you understand your personality type, you will be able to accomplish your real potential by letting go of all your negative traits. Clarity about your respective personality type can help you tune into the three wisdom centers – heart, belly and head.

Centuries ago, many ancient cultures had already recognized the importance of these three centers. In recent times, the neuroscientists have discovered the neurological networks in all these three areas, but what has the Enneagram got to do with the wisdom centers? Each of the nine personality types in the Enneagram is a combination of these three wisdom centers. You can try this test to know your type: check out the special gift you can find later in this book.

Introduction

This book will serve as a detailed guide on Enneagram, the ways it can be used to understand your potential, overcome your flaws and acknowledge your underlying characteristics. The chapters in the book will concentrate on what Enneagram is, how it works and how it can be used.

I hope this book serves as an informative and interesting read to you!

Happy Reading!

Chapter One:
Enneagram

If you are someone who is interested in taking your personal growth and awareness level to the next stage, then *the Enneagram of Personality (*also referred to as Enneagram*)* is essential for you. So, what is this Enneagram all about?

It is the psychological classification model that concentrates on your personality traits. It is similar to the popular Myers Briggs model. The Myers Briggs model helps in understanding your cognitive functions, whereas the Enneagram helps in creating awareness on your main personality traits (both at a conscious and subconscious level). It will help you know more about your individual traits and the unconscious strategy that you usually apply while taking decisions. It provides you a way to observe your ego mechanisms and personality patterns more closely. This cannot be easily done and requires practice in a mindful state.

What is an Enneagram?

An Enneagram is a powerful means for you to make a collective and personal transformation. The term *Enneagram* is derived from the two Greek words *Ennea* and *Grammos* – *Ennea* means *nine* and *Grammos* means *a written symbol*. The diagrammatic representation of Enneagram is a nine-pointed symbol that represents the nine distinctive strategies that relate self, the world and the others.

Each of the nine Enneagram types has a specific pattern of feeling, thinking and acting that basically stems from the outside view or inner drive. The Enneagram promotes a better and clear understanding through a universal language that rises above culture, religion, gender and nationality. Although we are all unique in our own ways, we mostly share common experiences rooted from different causes or scenarios.

Eventually, the Enneagram is an *inside job* that determines your type and helps you recognize your focus on your own understanding, core beliefs, development path and coping strategies. The fundamental value of the Enneagram comes from identifying the depth of your behavioral patterns and the way it relates to your focus of impulse, personal experience and awareness. It is not just based on your external behaviors, but has more to do with your internal mold.

The diagrammatic representation of the Enneagram structure might look complicated, but it is actually quite simple. Here is how it goes:

Draw a circle. Mark nine points at equal distances on its circumference. Assign each point by a number – 1 to 9. Let nine be at the top for uniformity and by rule. Each of these nine points represents the nine basic personality types. You will also need to connect all the nine points with each other through the inner lines of the Enneagram. You should connect the points in the following way:

- Points 3, 6 and 9 will have to form an equilateral triangle.

- Point 1 connects with 4, 4 with 2, 2 with 8, 8 with 5, 5 with 7 and 7 with 1.

- The six points (1, 4, 2, 8, 5, and 7) will form an irregular hexagram.

Your Enneagram structure will look like the one given below:

You may want to know more

This book, "Embrace Your Potential and Overcome Your Weak Points", is focused on the usage of the Enneagram through exercises, meditations and questions so you can utilize Enneagram for self-discovery and personal growth. With this book you are reading right now, you will know yourself better and will have more information about how your strengths and weaknesses impact your life.

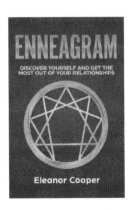

ENNEAGRAM

In case you haven't read it, I'd like to introduce my first book: "Enneagram: Discover Yourself and Get the Most Out of Your Relationships". This book serves as an excellent comprehensive guide to Enneagram for anyone who is a beginner and wants to discover the topic or knows character and personality types well but desires a new, fresh viewpoint.

Visit
https://www.amazon.com/dp/B07CVMQBF5/
to check out the book on Amazon.

Chapter Two:
Explore the Nine Types

The nine Enneagram types describe the personality and behavioral patterns of an individual. Concentrating on the three important elements (the psychological aspect, spiritual aspect and somatic aspect) helps to understand your personality better and paves way for a positive development structure. We will see more about these three elements in the next chapter.

There are three other centers of perception and intelligence when it comes to knowing your strengths and weaknesses:

- Head (The Intellectual Center)

- Heart (The Emotional Center)

- Body (The Instinctual Center)

Although every one of us experiences all three, each Enneagram personality type has a *home base* in one of them, or maybe a specific strength that associates with one of them. This prime center persuades the way you live in this world. It is the key factor that helps you to develop your potential and overcome the blind spots. When you balance all the three centers, it helps in achieving a well-balanced and peaceful life.

Head (The Intellectual Center)

The Enneagram types – 7, 6 and 5 form the head center, which is also referred to as the *Intellectual Center*. People belonging to this type are the *thinking-types* who mostly gather information, figure out things, have ideas and are rational, while taking decisions before they get ready to act. They primarily focus on creating safety and certainty, or work to find multiple alternatives (just in case one doesn't work).

Type 7 – The Epicure

7s believe that it is necessary to keep your possibilities open and be optimistic to lead a good life; therefore, they are adventurous and look for pleasurable options. They often like to stay unattached to avoid pain and concentrate on their own self.

Attention focus

- Glamorous future plans.

- Multiple options (to be on a safer side).

Lessons for life

- To regain and accept life's pleasures and pains as in the present moment.

Style of Speaking

- Spontaneous, high-spirited, idea-oriented, logical and fast-paced.

- Perceived by others as people who keep making excuses, who are apathetic to other's views, quick in shifting topics and always self-absorbed.

Type 6 – The Loyal Skeptic

6s believe that it is necessary to have constant vigilance to live in the hazardous world that can never be trusted. According to them, safety and certainty are important to lead a peaceful life; therefore, they are excellent in problem-solving. They can be trustworthy, intuitive, curious and good friends, but they are equally snappish, apprehensive and suspicious.

Attention focus

- They think about the worst-case scenarios.

- Work on options to deal with those scenarios.

Lessons for life

- To reclaim trust in self and others.

- Live comfortably, even when there is uncertainty.

Style of Speaking

- Information-oriented, attentive, quizzical and engaging.

- Perceived by others as people who are negative, opposing, demanding, skeptical or challenging.

Type 5 – The Observer

5s believe that it is necessary to safeguard self from a world that is too demanding but gives very little; therefore, they are happy with whatever they have. They are logical, modest and thoughtful. They can also be private and completely detached and refuse to give in easily.

Attention focus

- Intellectual understanding and gathering knowledge.

- Work to do away with the potential interference from other's feelings, agendas and desires.

Lessons for life

- To reconnect to the energy of your life force and understand your deepest feelings.

- To realize the availability of the surplus resources and abundant energy in the world.

Style of Speaking

- Not interested in *small talks*.

- Clear, verbose, methodical and focused on the content.

- Perceived by others as people who are distant, detached, emotionally disconnected and over-analytical.

Heart (The Emotional Center)

The Enneagram types – 2, 3 and 4 form the heart center, which is also referred to as the *Emotional Center*. They are high on feelings and mostly have concern and compassion for others, and they believe in loyalty and romance and therefore give special attention to the heart for negative and positive feelings.

Type 2 – The Giver

2s believe that it is important to give wholly to others to be loved; therefore, they are relationship-oriented, accommodating, kind and supportive, but they can also be equally demanding, haughty and interfering.

Attention focus

- Needs, desires and feelings of others.

Lessons for life

- To develop the humbleness by allowing yourself to be loved without being too needy.

- Having your own needs and working to fulfill them.

Style of Speaking

- Open, friendly, communicative, responsive to others' needs, supportive and approachable.

- Perceived by others as people who are irksome, indignant, controlling or overly helpful.

Type 3 – The Performer

3s believe that it is important to be successful and accomplish something in your life to be loved; therefore, they are mostly goal-oriented, fast-paced, competent and hard-working. They can also be intolerant, unmindful to feelings and are always driven by success.

Attention focus

- Goals, tasks and appreciation for accomplishments.

Lessons for life

- To understand the truth that love doesn't have anything to do with success or material wealth.

- You attract love, not because of *what you do,* but because of *who you are.*

Style of Speaking

- Confident, undeviating, fast-paced, excited and topic-focused.

- Perceived by others as people who are impatient, preventive, dominant to others' views and overly efficient.

Type 4 – The Romantic

4s believe that it is possible to regain an ideal state or get back the lost love by finding a situation or love that is special, gratifying and unique; therefore, they are genuine, idealistic, and compassionate and are deeply emotional. They can also be grumpy, self-absorbed and dramatic.

Attention focus

-   The missing factor (their quest for what is missing in their life).

Lessons for life

-   To regain fullness by appreciating what is there in the present moment instead of overthinking on what happened in the past, or will be happening in the future.

-   Accepting self as who you are without the need to be unique or special.

- Feeling the experience in your mind and body.

Style of Speaking

- Focused on self, too personal, expressive of feelings, and appreciate originality.

- Perceived by others as people who are too expressive, have deep emotions and are not completely satisfied with responses.

Body (The Instinctual Center)

The Enneagram types – 8, 9 and 1 form the body center, which is also referred to as the *Instinctual Center*. They are the *body-based types* who mostly focus on social belonging, power, personal security and taking the right action.

Type 8 – The Protector

8s believe that it is necessary to be influential and tough to assure safety and protection in the tough world; therefore, they are strong, action-oriented and straightforward. They like to be fair and seek justice whenever something goes wrong. They can also be reckless, extreme and too impactful.

Attention focus

- Getting things moving in the right direction at work or otherwise.

- Ensure others don't control them.

- Injustice.

Lessons for life

- To harness the life force in creative ways.

- Being assertive and vulnerable at the same time. Integrating both the attribute positively.

Style of Speaking

- Firm, commanding, honest, energetic and oriented to justice and truth.

- Perceived by others as people who are loud, dominating, intimidating and challenging.

Type 9 – The Mediator

9s believe that it is necessary to blend in and go with the flow to be valued and loved; therefore, they are steady, comprehensive, comfortable, friendly and easygoing. They look for harmony, but they can also get stubborn, be absentminded and evade things to avoid conflicts.

Attention focus

- External environment.

- Agendas of others (people around you).

Lessons for life

- To reclaim self.

- Wake up to your own priorities and concentrate on them.

Style of Speaking

- Friendly, focused on others' feelings and facts. They don't deal with situations aggressively.

- Perceived by others as people who are unclear, wavering, scattered and overly appeasing.

Type 1 – The Perfectionist

1s believe that it is necessary to be right and perfect to be worthy; therefore, they are responsible, self-controlled and hard working. They prefer to improve themselves based on the feedback or suggestion they receive. They can also be bitter, self-judging and critical.

Attention focus

- What is correct or incorrect – the right and the wrong.

Lessons for life

- To change things that can be changed and to accept things that cannot be changed.

- To develop the wisdom to know the difference between the acceptable and unacceptable.

Style of Speaking

- Direct, honest, specific, clear and always concentrates on the required details.

- Perceived by others as people who are closed-minded, judgmental and fixated on their opinions.

A special gift for you

Do you know which Enneagram type are you?

Now that you've become acquainted with the nine types, I happily introduce you to the bonus content I've put together to give you along with this book.

Visit http://eepurl.com/dtlgxf to download the Enneagram Test.

With this test, you will learn your type in just a few minutes.

Chapter Three:
Personality Development

The Enneagram is the focal point for the three key aspects of personality development:

- Psychological (Mental or Emotional aspects)

- Spiritual (Receptiveness)

- Somatic (Instinctual neuro-pathways)

When you work on these three elements individually, you add a lot of value to your traits and underlying behavioral patterns. The Enneagram serves as a map for you to work on all these areas that create an interaction with your own self. This greatly helps in increasing the effectiveness, while working on your personality.

Type 1

Psychology

- Strong inner critic.

- Holds back his/her desires and needs.

- Outburst of anger or guilt over behaviors or impulses that they review as wrong.

- Idealistic.

- Put forth a great effort to improve the world around them.

- May come forward to work for a political or a social cause (might take on the social reformer's role).

Spirituality

- To embrace the intrinsic perfection in one's own self and in the world.

- Attain tranquility by accepting the mistakes as a natural way to grow and learn.

- Important to relax by shifting the focus from the necessity to correct every mistake (of others) to *accepting* the errors, desires, differences and the darkness.

Somatics

- A lot of physical energy.

- Ability to exercise self-control over their impulses and feelings.

- This causes physical tension in the neck, jaw, shoulders, pelvic floor and diaphragm.

Type 1 has an instinctive ability to know their belly centers, but not consciously. This is because they usually hold the tension in the diaphragm causing a hindrance in breathing.

Type 2

Psychology

- Empathize with the feelings and needs of others.

- Alert on relationships and are good to others by being supportive.

- Face difficulty in turning attention towards self and own needs.

- Emotionally sensitive.

- Want to be liked and accepted by everyone and will be willing to change themselves to get this approval.

- Challenge in setting boundaries for self.

Spirituality

- To reclaim freedom from a world that will only love and approve people if their own needs are fulfilled.

- Should learn to pay attention to one's own needs.

- Should be ready to receive from others and give only what is right.

They can experience pure joy and happiness only if they are able to give and accept love freely.

Somatics

- Energetic and expressive in the upper body.

- Difficult to sense the lower body or stay grounded.

- Talk out to release the controlled emotions and anxiety (vocally expressive).

- Show empathy to others and are receptive to their feelings.

- May restrict breathing while waiting for other's responses (while waiting for an answer or decision).

Type 3

Psychology

- Ability to take the initiative and work hard to achieve their goals to succeed.

- Highly adaptive in nature and can meet the expectations of others.

- Extremely active. Have difficulty in slowing down.

- More inclined towards material benefits and praises.

- Doesn't concentrate much on inside emotions and feelings that can be a danger to themselves.

Spirituality

- Important to remember that they are human beings and not robots without emotions and feelings.

- Need to take steps to allow their feelings to surface.

- Open up to receive love and accept who they are.

Somatics

- Holds the tension or energy in the heart area.

- Instead of giving time to their feelings, they channel it to achieve productivity by getting into action for gaining results.

- Although the emotional pressure bottles up, the lid is still on.

- Have a strong life force, but will be unable to access it unless they are given an *external push*.

- Not slowing down to feel the natural pace in their body (especially tensions in the chest area).

Type 4

Psychology

- Experience a sense of yearning or feel distressed or envy for what is missing.

- Look for depth and intensity in relationships or work.

- Always on a mission to seek their inner personal creativity.

- Most 4s are artists who are pro in expressing the universal emotions.

- Should balance grief with joy and satisfaction in order to heal self.

Spirituality

- Need to realize the importance of appreciation and acceptance.

- Should live in the present moment.

- Must understand the significance of accepting things from the inside out and not the outside in.

Somatics

- Have an emotional life, which can lead to immense pain or extreme happiness.

- Oscillate between *striving hard to get recognized* and *getting lost in their own internal world.*

- Can easily get upset and withdraw self.

- On the contrary, they tend to open up when excited or anxious or have too many feelings.

Type 5

Psychology

-   Highly intellectual and knowledgeable.

-   Looks for privacy as the presence of other people might be too intruding.

-   Detached from emotional pressure.

-   Stays away from others and gives them freedom, but, at times, they feel lonely too.

-   Need to balance their withdrawal trait by reaching out to others, even if it involves conflict or embarrassment.

Spirituality

-   5s usually disengage themselves from emotional needs and feelings by withdrawing into the mind and reducing their needs.

- Reversing the process of *getting disengaged from the emotional self* is crucial.

- They can naturally hail the life energy by opening up their emotions and expanding the connection for their greater good.

Somatics

- Look to develop their expertise and improve their knowledge by protecting their independence and privacy.

- Always stay within their heads by setting aside the emotional needs or bodily sensations.

- Holds the tension in the gut region.

- Sensitive to touch, intrusion and sound.

Type 6

Psychology

- 6s use their intellect and perception to figure out people's character.

- Ability to perceive the world in a logical sense.

- Concentrates on safeguarding their community, group or project.

- Good at foreseeing problems and finding solutions.

- Keep oscillating between faith and doubt. Can be a true believer or a rebel.

- Tend to worry, put things off, get cautious and waver when anxious.

- When ready to face the cause of anxiety, they support themselves and get ready to act in order to conquer their fears.

- They can be more courageous and flexible when they learn to trust their instinct, even when there is an air of doubt or uncertainty.

Spirituality

- Got to get rid of doubt and fear by emphasizing the fact that the world is not such a threatening place to live.

- Journey to faith can be difficult, but it is a necessity.

Somatics

- Perceptive in foreseeing problems, identifying solutions and ascertaining rules for safety.

- Few are cautious, while others are in a hurry to act.

- Always on high alert mode when they sense danger signals (can be magnified, real or imaginary).

- They withdraw physically or mentally from situations that put them into an anxious mode.

- Build up rigidity and muscular tension leading to breathing issues.

- Throat and diaphragm are the control centers and 6s can have a problem in speaking (they tend to stutter) when anxious.

Type 7

Psychology

- Positive and optimistic with no limitations.

- Love to have fun while traveling and seek more adventure.

- Tend to get irritated or start criticizing when reality doesn't match with their ideologies.

- Challenging to concentrate on work or a relationship, as they cannot focus on the depth and intensity of the bond.

- Will need to balance themselves by slowing down and listening to other's suffering and their own (as well). Should be tolerant.

Spirituality

- Should welcome all walks of life and live in the present.

- Need to acknowledge both extremities of emotions equally – *grief, frustration, pain, boredom, fear* and *happiness, pleasure, options, and excitement.*

- Should be more empathetic with others and show gratitude.

Somatics

- Over-energetic and highly attentive.

- Experience looseness in shoulders and upper chest as the body concentrates more on avoidance (as patterns).

- The biggest challenge is to stay grounded as they often retreat from grief or pain by withdrawing into their minds.

Type 8

Psychology

- Have leadership quality as they take charge of situations.

- Fair on judging.

- Should control their excessive appetites.

Spirituality

- Should embrace virtue in people and approach every situation with an open mind.

- Should appreciate the inner truth in everyone.

- Need to learn to restrain the unlimited instinctual energy and delay the tendency to always jump into action.

Somatics

- Excellent instinctual energy.

- Always gets into the tough mode to avoid vulnerability.

- Shows chronic patterns of physical tension.

Type 9

Psychology

- Seeks harmony.

- Excellent in seeing all the perspective of life, but have a problem with inertia.

- Faces difficulty in setting priorities.

- Keep changing directions or shifting attention (they are constantly on the move).

Spirituality

- Should work towards awakening their inner self and get lively, especially during times of distress.

- Should set their own priorities and work towards the same within timelines.

- Avoid falling for secondary search (wavering) and resist from getting influenced by others.

Somatics

- Not in sync with their bodies.

- Not paying attention to the intuition that is operating in the gut.

- Holding tension in the body.

- Prefer staying undercharged and lack muscle tone.

- Low-energy individuals suffer from sluggishness and inertia, while high-energy individuals are super-active.

Chapter Four:
How does it work

You can look at the Enneagram as a set of nine distinct personality types. Each number on the Enneagram denotes one type, but it is quite common to find little of your self in almost all the nine types. But the point is, one of these nine types will stand out to be the closest to who you really are, and this becomes your *basic personality*.

You have one of these nine types dominating your personality, your inborn character and other pre-natal elements as the main determining factors of your type from childhood. Consequently, this inherent attitude fundamentally conditions the way you learn to adapt to the early childhood atmosphere; therefore, the overall course of one's personality mirrors the totality of all the childhood factors that helped in influencing its development. This includes the genetic factor as well.

How does the Enneagram work?

You need to have a basic understanding of how the Enneagram works before you try to determine your personality type. The Enneagram is basically a system with its structure represented in the form of a circle. There are arrows inside the circle that point in all the directions. The Enneagram depicts the nine personality types (ego structures) and all types are interconnected in different ways.

As mentioned earlier, each individual has a dominant type that is established in his/her childhood. It can also be before or after birth, but the definition is not clear yet. David Daniels, a famous Enneagram expert, tells that it is a combination – the type gets established both pre and post birth.

Along with the primary type, there is also a dominant wing attached to each individual and this can be one of the two types, i.e., the types on adjacent sides of the dominant wing. For instance, type 8 can be type 8 with a 9 wing or type 8 with a 7 wing. It is the wing that flavors the type. It is possible to examine your ego mechanisms in a solid way using the Enneagram.

The connection between the types doesn't end here – each will have a *stress point* (the individual will resemble this type when he or she is under stress). They also have an *integration type* (the individual will resemble all the healthy characteristics when they learn to manage the unhealthy aspect of their own type). You cannot be a pure personality type – there will be a unique mixture of your basic type and your wing type. Your basic type will dominate your overall personality, while the wing type will complement it by adding significant elements to your whole personality (which can be conflicting in some cases). You can consider your wing to be *the second side of your personality*. You will be in a better position to understand your own self only if you take both the basic type and wing type into consideration.

Wing Points and Dynamic Points

Two kinds of movement (each with a different quality) happen on the Enneagram. The movement that happens around the circumference of the circle to the points on the adjacent side of your personality type is referred to as *Wing Points*. The movement that happens inside the Enneagram to the two points that connect to your own point by a straight line is referred to as *Dynamic Points*.

Wing Points

The two points next to your own point (the home base) on the circumference of the circle are your neighbors whom you can visit easily. It naturally doesn't take much time to accept the personal style of your wing points. Although they are different from your *home base*, they are not very different, thereby allowing you to see the world through their eyes, or adapt to their habits (good and bad). When you are discovering your personality type for the first time, you might identify with both or one of your wings. It might also confuse you to the extent that you may not be able to distinguish between your basic type and wing type. This is because every type can be outlined as a combination of two wing points.

For instance, if you blend a 2 and a 4, you will come up with a 3 and, similarly, if you blend a 5 and a 7, you might end up with a 6. The point is, you can have access to both your wings and they can be helpful to you at various times with their different set of characteristics and resources. Nevertheless, some evidence confirms that one of the two wings is predominant or more recognizable. You will need to observe self to find out if you have a predominant wing or you keep moving to both the wings equally.

Regardless of the patterns, it is evident that your basic personality type is greatly influenced by your wings. This leads to various major behavioral fluctuations and changes in your perspective. This can also give you interesting variations amidst the nine types.

Dynamic Points

The movement that happens inside the Enneagram is not easy when compared to the movements that happen in your wing points. The movement that happens within the Enneagram causes a major shift in your experience – it can be temporary, but the change has a high impact on your behavioral pattern.

You will be able to notice the change in yourself, and most often people around you will notice it too. At times, these shifts can be distressing for you as you might think that you are no longer able to take control of your emotions or your behavioral patterns, but, when you start noticing these shifts and make necessary attempts to manage them well, they then can add value to your professional and personal development.

Chapter Four: How does it work

When you get access to an entirely new set of resources that can add value to your character or balance your existing personality, then you are benefitted by the change.

Moving to the dynamic points can help you in the following ways:

- You are ready to step out of the box.

- You willingly expand your options.

- You don't get stuck to your habitual style.

- You develop a whole new style to respond to the world around you.

Regardless of you being in the inner triangle (with connecting points 9, 6 and 3) or on the other set of lines (with connecting points 1, 4, 2, 8, 5 and 7), you will find two lines connecting your type to two other points. For instance, if you are type 8, then you will have connecting lines to type 2 and type 5.

In the *forward* direction, you have your *resource point or the stress point* and in the other direction (*moving back*), you have your *heart point* or *the relaxation point.*

The <u>resource point</u> is where you get to access some of the important qualities that help you to take action – you either go to that point when you are under stress, or you go there to access the competencies and intelligence of that point. Either way, you get stressed or uncomfortable when you go to the *resource point, which* is why it is also known as *the stress point.*

The <u>relaxation point</u> is where you get to occupy a type that is extremely helpful for your transformation and personal growth. This is the point that holds the key to most of your underlying personality issues, often termed as the *undeveloped side* or *the shadow side.* You will have to let down your usual defenses and relax in order to open up. You should let go of your normal way of looking at the world and try to be more vulnerable and flexible to allow *the new dimension* inside you. You are able to dwell deeper within you and learn more about *your real self* when you feel secure and safe. This makes you to be more available to your loved and intimate ones.

It is indeed challenging to get in touch with the inner feelings and core issues in your relaxation point. There is a possibility to get snapped back to your personality type when you continue with the usual operating procedures and go with the familiar point of view. However, if you are able to stay long enough in your relaxation point and incorporate the essence, then you will be able to re-inhabit your personality type with more balance.

ENNEAGRAM

You move *forward* to your *resource point (stress point)* in one of the following ways:

- 3 goes to 9, 9 goes to 6 and 6 goes to 3, i.e., 3963.

- 1 goes to 4, 4 goes to 2, 2 goes to 8, 8 goes to 5, 5 goes to 7 and 7 goes to 1, i.e., 1428571.

Similarly, you move *backwards* to your *relaxation point (heart point),* i.e., in the opposite direction:

- 3 goes to 6, 6 goes to 9 and 9 goes to 3, i.e., 3693.

- 1 goes to 7, 7 goes to 5, 5 goes to 8, 8 goes to 2, 2 goes to 4 and 4 goes to 1, i.e., 1758241.

Did you enjoy this book so far?

Let me stop you for a moment.

I believe that anyone can improve the quality of their life by becoming aware of their and other's driving forces. So they'll not only know the differences in the way people see the each other but can also accept it and use it for the benefit of their own and for others.

We are in a world full of diversity, surrounded by people with unique personalities, talents, motivations, and minds. I know that Enneagram helps to see and understand yourself and this world we live in. Both my experiences and experiences of others I've worked with prove that knowing the nine types helps you in all kinds of life situations. From self-discovery, to accepting and dealing with others Enneagram helps you to get the most out of it.

I believe that there are people reading this book that will be able to improve their lives and make a difference because of my work and effort. I'm not a self-development guru or a famous idol. I'm chasing neither the fame nor the money. As a self-publisher, my mission, my personal legend is to use the knowledge and talents I have to take my part of making the world a better place.

I'm asking your help to achieve this goal. If you enjoy this book and agree with my vision, please take a moment to visit Amazon.com and leave an honest review. I'd greatly appreciate it and it would help my work to get these ideas to more who seek it. Thank you very much!

Visit
https://www.amazon.com/dp/B07F5HHYQT/
to leave a review on Amazon.com!

Eleanor Cooper

Chapter Five:
How to get started

Each Enneagram type has a *forgotten or repressed* intelligence and a *supporting or primary* intelligence. The major step towards your self-development will be to reintegrate the *repressed center*. You have suppressed your *forgotten intelligence* from your conscious self since your early age. This is similar to the *Dynamic Point* theory of your *undeveloped (shadow) side in the relaxation point*. (Refer to Chapter 4.)

Your *repressed center* obstructs everything by controlling the whole show from the unconscious (or subconscious) level. For instance, if you have a repressed *thinking center (intellectual center)*, you get habituated to a particular routine and become arrogant. Similarly, if you have a repressed *feeling center (emotional center)*, you get dominated by misguided and silly emotions. Lastly, if you have a repressed *doing center (instinctual center)*, your actions are mostly misdirected.

The following table gives you a clear picture on the *repressed center* for your particular Enneagram type:

Enneagram Type	Repressed Center
Type 1 – The Perfectionist	Thinking (Intellectual) center – Head
Type 2 – The Giver	Thinking (Intellectual) center – Head
Type 3 – The Performer	Feeling (Emotional) center – Heart
Type 4 – The Romantic	Doing (Instinctual) center – Body
Type 5 – The Observer	Doing (Instinctual) center – Body

Type 6 – The Loyal Skeptic	Thinking (Intellectual) center – Head
Type 7 – The Epicure	Feeling (Emotional) center – Heart
Type 8 – The Protector	Feeling (Emotional) center – Heart
Type 9 – The Mediator	Doing (Instinctual) center – Body

You need to understand that your repressed center need not necessarily be clear from the way you interact with people. It is more to do with your inner world. For example, if *thinking* is your repressed center, you will most likely experience stagnancy while you think. It is more of your internal quality.

When you know your type's repressed center, you will need to take steps to bring them back to your conscious self. For instance, you will need to bring back your *repressed thinking center* by reading intellectual books and pushing yourself to take up ideas that ultimately challenge you. This way you will be able to *embrace your lost investigative side* and lose the *stagnancy in* the *thinking side*.

Similarly, you work on your *repressed doing center* by taking the risk to bring back your adventurous side. Likewise, you can work on your repressed feeling center by allowing yourself to experience all the emotions (especially negative ones) and acknowledging the discomfort. This way you allow yourself to feel the vulnerable side in you and work on understanding its effects on you.

Working on the Points

Point 1 – The Perfectionist

Wing Points

1s have two wings – 9 and 2.

Predominant 9 wing

- Oriented towards balance and harmony.

- 1s drive to get things right gets mediated by the desire to be comfortable.

- Tend to calm down by adopting a slow pace.

- Drawback: 9 wing can set the 1s to be flexible or less adaptable to others' needs.

- Advantage: Steady productivity with attention on quality.

Predominant 2 wing

- Drawn towards relationships.

- Being helpful and supportive.

- 1s are expressive when 2 wing is active.

- Drawback: Gets upset or anxious due to interpersonal conflicts or when others are not doing things right.

- Advantage: Perfect combination of organizational and people skills.

Dynamic Points

1s have two dynamic points – 7 (relaxation point) and 4 (resource point).

Relaxation point – 7

- Open to multiple possibilities.

- More tolerant towards multiple plans.

- Less judgmental and critical about self and others.

- 1s find it easier to go with the flow and have fun when they relax into the 7. Loosens the physical tension.

- In case the relaxation point is not integrated well, 1s tend to lose control and might indulge in excessive drinking habits.

- In case 1s succeed to integrate with 7, 1s hold the positivity and enthusiasm of the 7, along with the hard work and responsibility of their own point (1).

- Impulsiveness + Flexibility joins Thoughtfulness + Integrity.

Resource point – 4

- Emotionally expressive at 4 when 1s are unable to control their feelings.

- Bottled up emotions, or emotions that were held back for long, now starts spilling out.

- Drawback: Stress and the overwhelming feeling might lead to a hurtful or riotous way of opening up.

- When the 1s move to 4, they get to know how they feel and what they need which works mostly in their favor.

Point 2 – The Giver

Wing Points

2s have two wings – 1 and 3.

<u>Predominant 1 wing</u>

- Natural trait of 2s gets balanced (with 1 wing) by the need to *get things right*.

- More controlled and organized.

- Tend to get thoughtful by balancing their emotional side with self-discipline and the need to analyze the situations.

- Drawback: Physical tension and inner conflict. 2s get uncomfortable if they have to be perfect all the time (which is the trait of wing 1).

- Advantage: 1s self-containment and 2s outgoing energy give an efficient and steady style.

<u>Predominant 3 wing</u>

- Meet the expectations of others to become professionally successful.

- Flexible, hard working and responsive.

- Drawback: Will have to slow down to avoid losing energy fast as 2s are not the real 3s. Will also face difficulty in bringing attention to their own feelings and needs.

- Advantage: Activeness of 3 wing can make 2s excellent performers and efficient communicators.

Dynamic Points

2s have two dynamic points – 4 (relaxation point) and 8 (resource point).

<u>Relaxation point – 4</u>

- More attentive to their inner self unlike the 2s usual style of paying more attention to others.

- Ability to feel their emotions and inner needs.

- 2s might get stuck in the melancholy or grief state similar to the 4s when they try to find *the missing factor*.

- Ability to know what they really want can help the 2s to develop the emotional intensity.

- Successful integration of the 2s with the 4s can help to balance the emotional and external connection. They can find a *home within their self*.

Resource point – 8

- Making this a productive position entirely depends on how the 2s manage the 8s (as they are quite the opposite).

- 2s usually go with the flow, while 8s take charge. Most 2s will have difficulty in moving to 8 and will do so only when there is a lot of external stress or pressure.

- If handled well, 2s can learn how to handle conflict from the 8s, as it doesn't come to the 2s naturally.

- 2s can also be able to set boundaries and develop the skill of saying *no* when they really want to.

Point 3 – The Performer

Wing Points

3s have two wings – 2 and 4.

Predominant 2 wing

- Tend to be engaging and warm.

- Ability to make a personal connection at work.

- Overall accomplishments will be accompanied by a successful relationship with the team.

- 3s usually have more people skills as they are more of an extrovert compared to the 2s.

- Drawback: Reinforcing dependency for external recognition and approval, which is common with both 2s and 3s, may lead to bad taste.

- Advantage: Influence of the 2 wing can help the 3s to get more skilled in managing and leading a large team.

Predominant 4 wing

- 3s have more access to their internal moods and emotions with the dominance of wing 4. This will encourage them to create their own personal agenda.

- May retreat from their busy work state to analyze their options and choices.

- Drawback: 3s can get into depression if they work too much on their personal feelings.

- Advantage: 2s, who are usually more into people orientation, can get influenced by wing 4 to focus on the intellectual content.

Dynamic Points

3s have two dynamic points – 6 (relaxation point) and 9 (resource point)

<u>Relaxation point – 6</u>

- 3s start to think about their relationships, desires and lives when they feel safe enough to take a break from their constant action.

- 3s with the 6 territory provide the ability to develop strategy, ask the right questions and understand the opposing forces that are basically necessary for long-term success. This works well for the ones who are in the leadership position.

- Instead of taking on goals and plans without rationale thinking, 3s at point 6 get motivated to make informed and logical decisions.

- Sometimes being at 6 can give 3s unusual experiences of doubt and fear, but these insecure or disturbed feelings are required as they confirm that they are working on their professional and personal development.

Resource point – 9

- Point 9 helps the 3s to develop the ability to see things from others' point of view and to bring people together on the task in an approachable fashion instead of being too directive or competitive which is the usual trait of 3.

- When 3s move into 9, they tend to slow down and listen to the rhythms of the body (to take rest when needed and get back to the active mode when ready).

- Stress and too much work can force the 3s to move into 9, leading them to become inert or static which is basically not their character.

- However, 3s can benefit from harmony and hold grounding qualities if they can move to 9 without much pressure or stress.

Point 4 – The Romantic

Wing Points

4s have two wings – 3 and 5.

Predominant 3 wing

- Turn their attention towards the world.

- Can be successful in business if the 4s work in synchronization with wing 3.

- 4s can blend in by putting aside too much of their individualism but, at the same time, leave their personalized touch in the presentation or style.

- 4s can meet the expectation of others, but there will be mild friction when it comes to balancing their inner world and social life as 4s are always *into their own inner world*.

- Drawback: 4s can get impatient with shallow or ordinary activities and will want to get into things that offer greater intensity. This may lead to a complaining mode, or it can push them to look for excellence in whatever they get their hands on.

<u>Predominant 5 wing</u>

- 4s tend to look for a lifestyle, which can offer a lot of privacy, or will look for jobs that give them enough time to turn their attention inwards. Example: Writers, scholars, artists and musicians will fit the band.

- 4s like to work in a workplace set-up, which will require minimum contact with others, although there is an inner feeling of being in a relationship with the others, but at a distance.

- Compared to the 4s with wing 3, 4s with wing 5 will not be too concerned about meeting their colleague's expectations or to the intricacy of interpersonal relationships.

- Drawback: They will be looked at as arrogant, weird or unfriendly people.

- Advantage: The creative skills of the 4s with wing 5 will make up for their lack of people skills.

Dynamic Points

4s have two dynamic points – 1 (relaxation point) and 2 (resource point).

ENNEAGRAM

Relaxation point – 1

- 4s become emotionally calm and physically grounded when they are appreciated and feel secure, as the gravitational center shifts to the belly center.

- Less moody and have fewer emotional swings.

- 4s moving to relaxation point 1 helps them to think practically with lower feelings of longing or gloominess.

- 4s start to stand up for self instead of feeling victimized. They get more stable with self-assertion and instinctual energy instead of impulsive, angry outbursts.

- 4s who are quick in criticizing others tend to look for improvement in others when they move to point 1, thereby making an effort to stay gracious and friendly.

Resource point – 2

- 4s on point 2 usually feel that they are stressing out self by staying nice for too long and will need to move forward for their own benefit.

- They also feel that they are losing their individuality by playing nice to gain personal connections and people's approval.

- However, if 4s are able to take it under control, point 2 can help them come out of their isolated state and connect with the outside world in a better way.

- 4s can try to choose this approach in a professional environment for a healthy work set-up, as being stuck in their own interior world might give assumptions to others.

Point 5 – The Observer

Wing Points

5s have two wings – 4 and 6.

<u>Predominant 4 wing</u>

-   5s with wing 4 have an active emotional
    life, which can influence their behavior
    and decision.

-   Integrating the feeling and thinking
    center is the challenge here – they
    shouldn't create conflict or pull them in
    different directions.

-   Drawback: Although wing 4 can support
    the 5s to develop better interpersonal
    warmth, it might also lead them to
    disorganized or unpredictable style.

-   This wing helps the 4s to emphasize more
    on improving relationships instead of
    getting into materialistic or scientific
    models.

- Compassion is more important when it comes to relationships; therefore, most 5s tend to get pulled towards this wing when they are looking for a personal connection, especially with partners or romantic interests.

Predominant 6 wing

- 5s with wing 6 will try to reinforce their mental center by focusing on the technical data, information and knowledge when it comes to solving life's challenges.

- Drawback: 5s tend to feel increased worry and fear, thereby magnifying the dangers and threats than they actually are. They may try to get detached or put up more boundaries.

- Advantage: Wing 6 helps in reinforcing the incredible ability of being insightful, thus giving space for creativity, which is a natural trait of the 5. 5s are loyal to a relationship, similar to the 6s.

Dynamic Points

5s have two dynamic points – 8 (relaxation point) and 7 (resource point).

<u>Relaxation point – 8</u>

- The shift of 5s when they move to point 8 can be dramatic – the quiet withdrawn 5 will suddenly become more expressive, assertive and body-based. This shifting paradigm can be challenging for their partner or friend.

- Both point 5 and point 8 are always self-centric, i.e., he or she keeps referring only about self. Listening and hearing the other person's viewpoint is always difficult.

- 5s in point 8 can have a lot of good positive energy when appropriately managed.

- It is incredible if the detached 5 is able to feel the grounding of point 8.

- 5s who pass through the line regularly (point 8) when they are into physical activities such as martial arts, sports or other outdoor action.

<u>Resource point – 7</u>

- The reserved 5s become more extroverted and outgoing when they move to point 7.

- 5s in this point can act in two different ways – they can be the life of the party and spread their vibrant energy everywhere, or they can be pressurized when talking to people.

- 5s can feel stressful being at 7 at such situations and will want to recoil and retreat to their own private space.

Point 6 – The Loyal Skeptic

Wing Points

6s have two wings – 5 and 7.

<u>Predominant 5 wing</u>

-   6s with wing 5 will want to preserve their confidentiality and privacy for security purposes.

-   May feel uncomfortable and aloof among people in social gatherings.

-   Knowledge is valued more than experience and they will want to figure out things before springing into action.

-   More emphasis is given to cognitive abilities.

-   Drawback: Have the tendency to put off decisions or postpone things that need visibility.

- 6s with wing 5 prefer structured and methodical situations and therefore might work as scholars, professors, scientists, teachers or writers.

- Sense of security depends on the relationship they have with friends and family.

- They tend to keep all the agreements (paperwork) in place.

- At times, they feel isolated or have mixed feelings towards people.

Predominant 7 wing

- 6s with wing 7 can be pushed to participate in adventures and have an enjoyable experience.

- Like the 7, 6s get excited to create interesting plans, but it is crucial to know their limits as the 6s always have their skeptical mindset.

- They try to engage others when it comes to discussing issues or ideas.

- 6s with wing 7 can be comprehensive but be too criticizing, be sociable but edgy.

- *Agree to disagree* – most 6s with this wing go by this.

- Group projects, group trips and group sports are mostly preferred.

Dynamic Points

6s have two dynamic points – 9 (relaxation point) and 3 (resource point).

Relaxation point – 9

- The shift of 6s to point 9 can be noticed when they drop their center of gravity to the belly. They accept things as it happens and often are less concerned about figuring out things.

- 6s usually foresee problems and question the motives of people, and are cautious in dangerous situations, but, when they move to point 9, all of this withers away.

- Point 9 makes them more relaxed, but if the 6s exert too much, they can end up with inertia (the problems faced by the 9s).

- When done the right way, 6s with point 9 can have a combination of an instinctual grounded feeling and insightful intellect.

- Most 6s with point 9 work out or get into athletics to evade the *bigger perspective of the mind*. This way they don't need to relax their mind and therefore tend to go with the flow (the usual style of 9).

Resource point – 3

- 6s with point 3 get to achieve their results quickly as they get into action mode immediately.

- No excessive thinking or doubting their own self.

- Instead of getting controlled by the intellect or rules of point 3, the energy of point 3 acts more adjustable and approachable for the 6s. This is more about meeting the expectations of the external factors.

- When it comes to business, 6s are pushed or pulled to the point 3. 6s can manage it to a point, but it can get stressful for them so, to avoid falling sick, it is necessary to get back to their home base (point 6).

Point 7 – The Epicure

Wing Points

7s have two wings – 6 and 8.

<u>Predominant 6 wing</u>

- 7s with wing 6 become more of the mental-types – they tend to always be within their heads by not concentrating on their emotional and bodily feelings.

- They have the ability to envision, think, plan and execute things at incredible alertness and mental speed.

- 7s incorporate the loyalty (character) of wing 6 in them.

- Moving to this wing can make them more committed to relationships, and also display a good rapport and understanding within the teams in a professional environment.

Predominant 8 wing

- 7s with wing 8 get attracted to physical and sensate experiences, and will want more adventure in their life (travel, extreme sports, party, business ventures, etc.).

- When both the home base and dominant wing are in the expansive mode, they can get too far into the world – it would be difficult finding them at home or being stuck in a cubicle in the office.

- They believe they can do whatever they dream.

- Drawback: This over-excitement and self-referencing can lead them to lose their grounding.

- Advantage: This quality makes them extremely creative leading to self-absorption, but, if they are ready to take accountability for a venture or work for someone apart from self, they can expand more and feel the joy.

Dynamic Points

7s have two dynamic points – 5 (relaxation point) and 1 (resource point).

Relaxation point – 5

- 7s feel secure and safe when they move to point 5. They also tend to correct their over-reactive self.

- Moving to point 5 makes the 7s to withdraw within self by going deep and silent. They tend to encounter frustration and fright in the process.

- Drawback: They feel lonely or get bored too soon.

- Advantage: Most 7s understand that getting centered within self can provide clarity in thoughts and perception, and it is good to withdraw once in a while and silence the mind from the gushing flow of activity outside.

- Since this is not how 7s usually are, they quickly get back to their normal self when people around ask – *why are you so withdrawn and silent?* But, if they are able to work well with point 5, they tend to get stronger by centering self, setting limits and making smart choices.

Resource point – 1

- The shift that happens when the 7s move to point 1 can be intense.

- 7s usually don't expect too much from the environment, but the traits of point 1 are that everything needs to be perfect.

- Moving to 1 can make the 7s more judgmental, critical and angry as they get stressed when they are pushed to make things right always.

- They change from '*All ok*' to '*You are not doing it right.*'

- If they are able to handle the shift properly, they get to incorporate the structures of point 1. They tend to get more systematic, organized, focused, get to the action and always look for options.

Point 8 – The Protector

Wing Points

8s have two wings – 7 and 9.

<u>Predominant 7 wing</u>

- 8s with wing 7 become more gregarious, amiable and charismatic.

- Similar to the 7s with wing 8, 8s with wing 7 will love to experience adventures, but unlike the 7s, 8s tend to be more physically grounded.

- They get incredible access to enthusiasm, dynamism and energy.

- Channeling the energy well will help the 8s become successful in any field – be it athletes, entrepreneurs, warriors, contractors or artists.

- Drawback: Since both 8s and 7s are self-referencing, they tend to always look out for self, rather than being considerate to others.

- Hearing the impact of their behavior on others can make them change.

Predominant 9 wing

- Wing 9 makes the 8s more laid back, making their energy levels a bit quieter.

- Instead of leading, they tend to work or exercise control from behind the scenes.

- 8s with wing 9 become obsessive as their aggressive quality gets bottled up inside and they get stuck with repeated behavioral patterns.

- Like the 9s, the 8s with this wing face trouble in getting things started, have low momentum and difficulty in changing directions.

- Drawback: The 8s with this wing start getting angry to get things moving and to escape from stillness.

Dynamic Points

8s have two dynamic points – 2 (relaxation point) and 5 (resource point).

Relaxation point – 2

- 8s get closer to their emotional center when they move to point 2.

- The usual caring and generous 8s tend to become open or vulnerable. In general, 8s keep their defenses and boldness strong to face a world filled with inconsistency and moving to point 2 can bring their tender and vulnerable side.

- It takes a lot of courage for them to open up.

- 8s in point 2 spend more time in the heart point, making them more gentle and caring (which the 2s are good at).

- They offer a different kind of intelligence while taking decisions, and tend to come out with positive energy.

Resource point – 5

- 8s who look for privacy almost regularly move to point 5, as even the 5s need their own space.

- 8s who usually take charge of situations tend to become quieter when in 5, allowing them to reflect on their thoughts and strategize accordingly.

- Since 8s are always into everything, moving to 5 can help them to detach and distance for some time.

- If not handled properly, 8s staying in point 5 for long can lead to depression as they tend to shut down completely.

Point 9 – The Mediator

Wing Points

9s have two wings – 8 and 1.

<u>Predominant 8 wing</u>

- 9s with wing 8 tend to show their angry, rebellious side, as 8s are usually more of a rebel.

- 9s get more assertive, but when managed well it helps them in their professional environment, especially in the leadership area.

- They willingly come forward to fight for justice and truth either the 9s way or the 8s way (angry explosion).

<u>Predominant 1 wing</u>

- 9s in wing 1 get perfect, organized, principled and methodical. The wing 1 can pull the 9s into their territory, such that it becomes almost impossible to differentiate the personality of a 9 from the 1.

- 9s take control of the situation, but try to get things done in harmony – be good, follow the rules and everything will fall into place.

- The usual rebellious 9s are compelled to abide by the expectations of *the influential figures (authority)* with wing 1 taking dominance.

- Being the actual 9, they often overcome the 1s role and show passive aggression by moving away or forgetting.

Dynamic Points

9s have two dynamic points – 3 (relaxation point) and 6 (resource point).

Relaxation point – 3

- 9s become more active in the feeling center, but at times it can get too overwhelming for them.

- 9s in point 3 are able to maintain a good connection in a relationship as unlike the usual way of 9s where they wait, think, sit on it before communicating, 9s in point 3 pushes them to decide faster.

Resource point – 6

- 9s who get motivated or pressurized by external events or face conflicts when they got to step out of their comfort zone, they move to point 6.

- 9s in point 6 can focus on the trouble spots instead of looking only at the issue that is disturbing them.

- Moving to point 6 helps them to differentiate between the various options and chart their action plan.

- Drawback: 9s in point 6 can get more fearful or anxious and sometimes are not familiar when it comes to handling critical situations.

Chapter Six:
Different options

Enneagram can be used as a therapeutic and a diagnostic aid to work on personal growth and development. When you accept your basic personality and dominant wing, you indirectly acknowledge the necessity to work on the underdeveloped areas. Integrating and incorporating the positives of a particular point (resource point or relaxation point) can help you grow better as a person. This is the natural and organic way of developing self.

How do you grow?

When you consciously implement the following by questioning self and start your quest for a better awakening, you create a win-win situation for self and for the others around you.

- Work on developing the underdeveloped wing (the less dominant wing). Although both your wings are active, one wing is more predominant compared to the other wing. You will need to work towards developing the *shadow persona* of self.

- You usually get fixated to a primary center (Thinking, Feeling, Instinctual (doing) centers), but try going counter-clockwise to the next center and develop that particular center within you.

- Try getting into the meditative state every day – this allows you to detach yourself from the habitual way of thinking. When you get into this non-thinking state and hold it for at least a few seconds, you will be able to grow the ability of detaching yourself from your normal life. A form of grounding! This allows you to observe your own self and find out *what you need from life*. You get into a calm and peaceful state of mind.

- When you are able to detach yourself, you can slowly develop your ability to shift your focus to the remaining 8 Enneagram types you inherently have but, again, don't overexert. Spend less time in the other 8 types. When you are successful in doing this, you tend to be more flexible and get the ability to make wise choices.

- Each Enneagram type has its own unique way of being present *in the moment,* i.e., mindfulness. Working on your type helps you grow!

Examples:

Enneagram Types	Mindfulness
Type 1	Attempting to achieve accuracy in work, environment and self.
Type 2	Serving and caring for

	others.
Type 3	Performing a role efficiently that leads to visible achievement.
Type 4	Exploring own individuality and distinguishing self from others.
Type 5	Observing any object of attention by getting into detached mode.
Type 6	Apprehending potential problems or dangers.
Type 7	Looking for experiences, possibilities and potential pleasures in the environment.
Type 8	Attempting to take control and achieve

	dominance over the environment.
Type 9	Bringing harmony to self, others and the environment

In this case, the environment can be external as well as internal. Exercising mindfulness will require one to lose self in the mindsets to achieve inner tranquility. It is not easy to practice mindfulness techniques as it takes a lot of practice. Spending a few seconds in meditation can help you overcome the hurdles you experience.

Sit down and focus on your breath – every single breath. Concentrate on your breath as you inhale and exhale. Let your mind be empty of thoughts. Your breathing should be your only focus.

It may be difficult initially, but with regular practice, you will gradually be able to gain momentum in your life.

You can try the following to achieve mindfulness depending on your Enneagram type:

Enneagram Types	How to work?
Type 1	Let go! Experience how it feels when you let go of your grudges, pain and negative emotions.
Type 2	Spend time with self. Look into you!
Type 3	Live the moment. Realize the importance of *being present*.
Type 4	Stay grounded. Feel it!
Type 5	Go for direct experiences. Realize the

	insight behind it.
Type 6	Feel your *feeling center*. Experience the comfort of you!
Type 7	Experience joy in the smallest things. Make the ordinary feel extraordinary!
Type 8	Feel how strong it is when you are not in control! Loosen up!
Type 9	Seek the harmony within you!

It is important to understand the blockage you face from within, acknowledge it, accept the barrier and then tell yourself you can do it despite the entire barrier. Don't be judgmental always! You do *push-ups* to strengthen your body, so, similarly, *meditate* to strengthen your mind. Anchor the ship by being its captain!

Conclusion

We have come to the end of this book. I would like to take this opportunity to thank you once again for choosing this book.

The book has covered the primary objective, which is to serve as a guide to help you identify your strengths and weaknesses based on your Enneagram types. The chapters take you on tour to all the nine Enneagram types, its nine points and three centers. They also focus on the positives and negatives of the type when they move into a particular wing point or dynamic point. It gives a quick brief on how to accept, acknowledge and work towards your personal growth.

I sincerely hope this book was useful and has helped in answering most of the queries you had in mind.

ENNEAGRAM

If you enjoyed this book, would you please take a minute and post an honest review of it on Amazon? I'd really appreciate it, as it will help me get these ideas out there to more people!

Visit the product page to leave a review on Amazon.com!
http://www.amazon.com/dp/B07F5HHYQT/

And if you forget to check the Enneagram Test I'm giving along with this book as a gift, you can get it here:
http://eepurl.com/dtlgxf

Thank you and best wishes!

Eleanor Cooper☐

Discover Yourself and Get the Most Out of Your Relationships

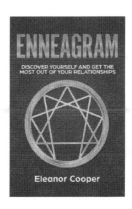

In case you haven't read it, I'd like to introduce my first book: "Enneagram: Discover Yourself and Get the Most Out of Your Relationships". This book serves as an excellent comprehensive guide to Enneagram for anyone who is a beginner and wants to discover the topic or knows character and personality types well but desires a new, fresh viewpoint.

Visit
https://www.amazon.com/dp/B07CVMQBF5/
to check out the book on Amazon.com!

32569804R00066

Made in the USA
Lexington, KY
04 March 2019